LEARNING MALAYALAM VOWELS MADE EASY

Written & Illustrated by
Dr. Abraham Thomas Eettickal

Cover Image by
Neva Thomas

അ
Ā

അരണ
Arana
Lizard

Colour in

അ ....

അ ....

അ ....

അ ....

അ ....

ঔ ....

ঔ ....

ঔ ....

ঔ ....

ঔ ....

ঔ ....

ঔ ....

ঔ ....

ঔ ....

ঔ ....

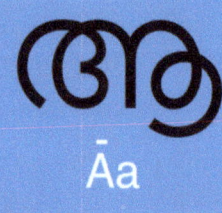

ആ
Āa

ആമ
Aama
Turtle

Colour in

ആ ....

ആ ....

ആ ....

ആ ....

ആ ....

இ
E

இல
Ela
Leaf

Colour in

இ ....
இ ....
இ ....
இ ....
இ ....

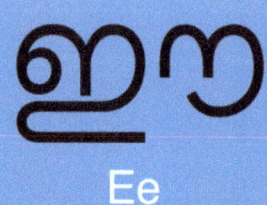

ഈ
Ee

ഈച്ച
Eecha
Fly

Colour in

ഈ ....

ഈ ....

ഈ ....

ഈ ....

ഈ ....

உ
U

உடுப்பு
Uduppu
Dress

Colour in

உ ....
உ ....
உ ....
உ ....
உ ....

ഊ
Uu

ഊഞ്ഞാൽ
Unjal
Swing

Colour in

ഊ ....
ഊ ....
ഊ ....
ഊ ....
ഊ ....

ඉරු
Eru

ඉරුතු
Erutu
Season

Colour in

ඉරු ....

ඉරු ....

ඉරු ....

ඉරු ....

ඉරු ....

എ
A

എലി
Ali
Rat

Colour in

എ ....

എ ....

എ ....

എ ....

എ ....

ഏ	Colour in
Aaa	
ഏണി	
Aani	
Ladder	

ഏ ....

ഏ ....

ഏ ....

ഏ ....

ഏ ....

I

ഐ

I
Eye

Colour in

ഐ ....

ഐ ....

ഐ ....

ഐ ....

ഐ ....

ഒ
O

ഒട്ടകം
Ottakam
Camel

Colour in

ഒ ....

ഒ ....

ഒ ....

ഒ ....

ഒ ....

ഓ
Oo

ഓട്ടം
Oottam
Run

Colour in

ഓ ....

ഓ ....

ഓ ....

ഓ ....

ഓ ....

ഔ
Ou

ഔഷധം
Oushadam
Medicine

Colour in

ഔ ....
ഔ ....
ഔ ....
ഔ ....
ഔ ....

അം
Am

അംഗം
Angam
Organ

Colour in

അം ....

അം ....

അം ....

അം ....

അം ....

അഃ

Aa

അഃ

Ahhh !!!
The end

അഃ ....

അഃ ....

അഃ ....

അഃ ....

അഃ ....

അ	ആ	ഇ
Ā	Āa	E

ഈ	ഉ	ഊ
Ee	U	Uu

ഋ	എ	ഏ
Eru	A	Aaa

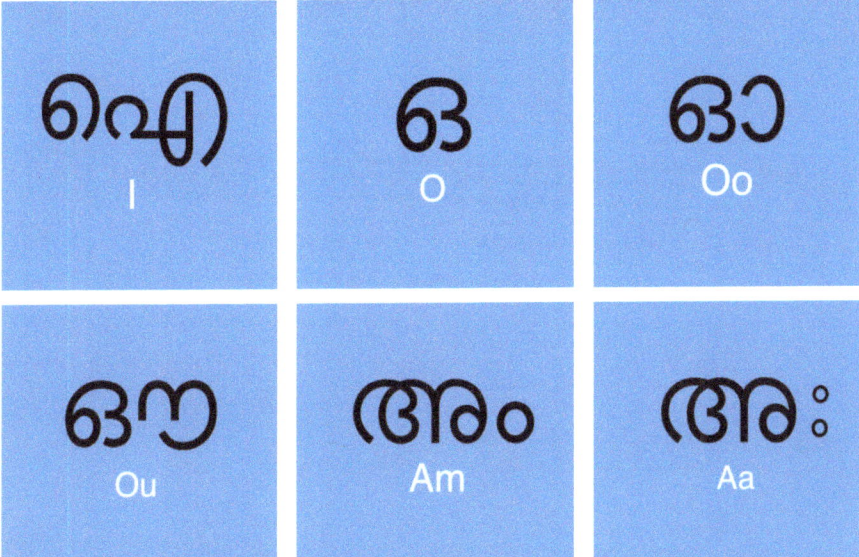

To my wonderful
Neva & Aiden

First published by LIGHT AUSTRALIA in 2021
ABN: 97813360788

Text and Illustrations copyright (c) Dr. Abraham Thomas, 2021.

Cover Image done by Neva Thomas

Dr. Abraham Thomas asserts his moral rights as the author and illustrator of this book.

Design and Layout by: Facebook.com/Grafixo

All rights reserved. Without limiting the rights under copyright reserved above, no part of this publication may be reproduced, stored in or introduced into a database and retrieval system or transmitted in any form or any means (electronic, mechanical, photocopying, recording or otherwise) without the prior written permission of the author, unless specifically permitted under the Australian Copyright Act 1968 as amended.

ISBN 978-0-6450541-5-6

Printed in Australia

NATIONAL
LIBRARY
OF AUSTRALIA

A catalogue record of this book is available from the National Library of Australia

www.ingramcontent.com/pod-product-compliance
Lightning Source LLC
Chambersburg PA
CBHW062024290426
44108CB00024B/2766